TO:

God

FROM:

A Woman's Heart

EVERYDAY PRAYERS

 **ZONDERVAN**®

To God; From a Woman's Heart
Copyright © 2009 by Zondervan

Requests for information should be addressed to:
Zondervan, *Grand Rapids, Michigan 49530*

ISBN 978-0-310-31852-1

Text excepted from A Little Book of Women's Prayer, Copyright © 1996, Marshall Pickering, and Women at Prayer, copyright 1994, Marshall Pickering. Used by permission.

All Scripture quotations, unless otherwise indicated, are taken from the Holy Bible; New International Version®, NIV® Copyright © 1973, 1978, 1984 by International Bible Society. Used by permission of Zondervan. All right reserved.

Interior Design by Gayle Raymer

Printed in China

09 10 11 12 • 5 4 3 2 1

FACING
A NEW
DAY

*L*ORD, YOU ARE WITH ME as
each new day dawns.
Give me your peace.

Lord, you are with me as I meet others.
Give me your loving ways.

Lord, you are with me as I go about my work.
Give me your understanding.

Lord, you are with me as I use my time.
Give me your compassion.

Lord, you are with me as I end my day.
Give me your forgiveness.

THE MOTHERS' UNION, ENGLAND

*L*ORD, help me to remember that
nothing is going to happen to me
today that you and I together cannot handle.

JOAN SHARPLES

*L*ORD, as we begin another day,
please guard and guide us on our
way. Help us to serve as best we can our
families, friends and fellow human beings, to
show our faith by love and prayer for others.
Grant, O Lord, that we may be always
faithful and true to you.

SUSANNA WRIGHT

$\mathcal{D}$EAR FATHER, we thank you for bringing us safely to a new day. May your Holy Spirit be with us in thought, word and deed, and guide us to do your will at all times.

MOTHERS' UNION, ENGLAND

DEAR FATHER, I awake each new dawn and wonder what is in store for me. I pray that you will travel along the road with me each day, whether it be rough or smooth. Lord, I put my life into your hands.

VIOLET REYNOLDS

*M*y Lord and friend, please help me through this day whatever it may bring. It is lovely having that feeling that you are by my side all the time; you help me in so many ways. Thank you for blessing and caring for me.

Iris Stubbington

*H*OLD MY HAND, LORD, as I enter each new day—may every step along the way be with you beside me; may every word I speak be spoken in accordance with your love; may my every action be guided by my awareness of your presence, so that as I come to evening I may lie down with peace in my heart, knowing that you are there.

ANTHEA TOFT

DEAR LORD AND SAVIOR, we thank you for taking care of us through the night. May we know and feel your presence with us through the day. May we know and feel your presence with us as we go about our daily work and know that you are helping and guiding us in all that we do.

EVELINE SELLERS

*H*EAVENLY FATHER, thank
you for this new day. Thank
you for the fulfillment of your promise and
commitment in the sunrise. Forgive me my
sins, show me your will for today and give me
your strength to do it.

JOAN WILKINS

*D*EAR LORD, we thank you for the dawning of each new day, bringing with it opportunities to serve you anew. Help us not to waste those opportunities but to take delight in your service hour by hour, remembering that you were the servant of all. Strengthen our faith and that of our loved ones each day by the power of your Holy Spirit, and when it is time to lie down and rest, my we be aware of your comforting presence.

DOROTHY ROBINSON

*D*EAR FATHER, may your presence be with me this day as I rise to comfort the baby and watch the departures for work and school.

Dear Father, may your presence be with me this day, as I clean the house and prepare the food.

Dear Father, may your presence be with me this day in the supermarket and in the neighborhood.

Dear Father, may your presence be with me this day as I put away the dishes and bandage a knee.

Dear Father, may your presence be in my home, in my deeds and in my heart, this day and every day.

SYLVIA LEONARD

*D*EAR LORD, as I open my eyes on another day, please accompany me on my way. Please grant me understanding and encourage me to do your will, so that when evening falls again you may grant me rest and quietness.

ST. ASAPH DIOCESE, WALES

*G*RANT, O LORD, that everyone
who has to do with me this day may
be the happier for it. May it be given me,
moment by moment , what I should say; and
may I have the wisdom of a loving heart to say
the right thing rightly. Keep me alive to the
feelings of others; give me the quick eye for
little kindnesses, that I may be ready in doing
them and gracious in receiving them. Give me
a quick perception of the needs of others and
may I be eager-hearted in helping them.

MARY PRITCHARD

• • •

BUSY,
BUSY

*L*ORD, you are with me as I use my time. Give me your compassion.

UNKNOWN

*A*LMIGHTY GOD, who gives
us strength to cope with the
stresses and details of our daily lives, grant us
the power of your Holy Spirit so that we may
be able to keep cheerful and calm, showing
your love to others.

MOTHERS' UNION, ENGLAND

•••
19

*L*ORD, I do not find you in the noise and bustle of my busy life but in the quiet moments, so teach me to pause more often and help me to hear your voice in the stillness.

JOYCE JENKINS

O GOD, OUR FATHER, God of mercy, love and grace, teach us to be still so that within the inmost center of our being we may know your presence. Teach us to be still that our minds may listen to your guidance. Teach us to empty our hearts of self so that you can fill them with yourself and make us channels through which your healing love will flow to those for whom we pray.

EILEEN BETHELL

ATHER, during our busy daily
lives teach us to be spontaneous
in worshipping you. Whenever we are
overwhelmed by the wonders of nature or
life itself let us be still and stand in awe and
gratitude and say "Thank you, Lord."

HAZEL FOUNTAIN

*S*LOW ME DOWN, LORD, ease the pounding of my heart by the quieting of my mind. Steady my hurried pace with the vision of the eternal reach of time. Give me amid the confusion of my day the calmness of the everlasting hills. Inspire me to send my roots deep into the soil of life's enduring values, that I may grow toward the stars of my greater destiny.

N.H.

WORK

$\mathcal{D}$EAR LORD, strengthen me to do
my tasks today, and though some
things are hard to do and some people hard
to understand, comfort me as you always do.

ELSIE MANSERGH

*H*OLY SPIRIT, I must make a
decision in the next few minutes.
Show me plainly what is God's will.

JOY HAWTHORNE

*L*ORD, you are in all the people I meet at work: the young mother, the woman with a smile on her face, the man with a joke on his lips. You are in me as I talk with people and pray that some of your love shows through in the things I say and in the look on my face.

ANNE RIMMER

*L*ORD, we bring to you the thousands who are unemployed, and those facing little hope of ever working again. We pray too for young people who have never known employment. Give them courage to face each new day. In your mercy, Lord, show us the way forward, guide our leaders, and help us to have pride in our work and in ourselves.

IRIS JUBBER

I'm starting work again tomorrow.
I'm excited God, but oh so scared!

May I find fulfillment in this venturing out.

Lord God, help me to keep a right balance
between family, home and work; help me
to keep my priorities right so our home will
continue to be a place of love and security.

JOINED IN LOVE, NEW ZEALAND

···

*L*ORD, I know you created me for a special purpose, to serve you in a unique way. You have given me a gift and talents, a certain something no one else has. Help me to be a valuable link in the chain of humanity; help me to find peace and meaning in what I do, knowing no one else can be me.

SALISBURY DIOCESE, ENGLAND

FATHER, I have been asked to
undertake something that I have
not done before. I feel unsure of my own
capabilities. I ask, "Why me?" Help me to
feel your presence near me, to guide and
encourage. Help me to know your will in this
and to use the gifts that you have given me.

CHELMSFORD DIOCESE, ENGLAND

*L*ORD, a lot of the work I have to do is dull, deadly dull. Sometimes I'm so bored and sometimes I'm depressed. It goes on day after day. God, sometimes I hate work. And then I remember two things and take heart; I ask your help to keep them more in mind.

I remember the carpenter's shop at Nazareth. That can't always have been joy and sunshine. People can be very rude to others who work for them, so I know that you understand and I'm thankful. I remember, too, that my work is linked to the work of others—to all people. They depend on me and I depend on them. Lord, keep me faithful.

MOTHERS' UNION, ENGLAND

*O*ur loving MASTER and God, we thank you for making us women, and for the joy of being a wife and/or mother. In these times, Lord, many women hold jobs or run businesses in addition to the arduous responsibilities of running their homes. We need your special grace and blessing to be able to be successful both at home and at work; we often neglect one for the other. Lord, help us to so organize and manage our time and homes that we will be able to progress at our various jobs. Give us the spirit and heart that is easily content with what has been given to us by you, so that we are not blinded by envy and selfish drive.

DR. S.O. MALOMO

•••

MARRIAGE

*L*ORD, we are so much in love and spend so much time thinking about each other. Help us not to be possessive, but to keep our wide circle of friends. Help us to grow to understand each other. Help our love not to blind us to differences that we must accept in our own individual uniqueness. We know we have to work at our relationship but we are tempted to think that everything will just fall into place and be wonderful. Help us to be open with each other, and let others share our great happiness.

CHELMSFORD DIOCESE, ENGLAND

*L*ord, guide those about to be married. Help them to face their future together with love, patience and understanding. Lead them through life with your love, and bring them richness and fulfillment.

Margaret Bloomfield

*L*ORD, in the day-to-day living of marriage may husbands and wives never take each other for granted. May their love remain strong to withstand the pressures of today's world. In times of stress or tension may they constantly find renewal in the strength of your love, and in times of joy to praise and bless your holy name.

PORTSMOUTH DIOCESE, ENGLAND

GOD, THANK YOU for this second
time of marriage. We each accept all
that has gone before. We pledge ourselves
to this new love. May our experiences and
differences take on a positive value, that
through them we may enrich our lives as we
learn from one another.

Thank you for our past, for the pains and for
the joys.

Thank you for your blessing on us now. May
we continue to know this blessing and may it
always be part of our lives together.

JOINED IN LOVE, NEW ZEALAND

*L*ORD, HELP US TO REMEMBER when we first met and the strong love that grew between us. Help us to work that love into practical things so nothing can divide us. We ask for words both loving and kind, and for hearts always ready to ask forgiveness as well as to forgive.

Dear Lord, we put our marriage into your hands.

ANN FRY

O GOD, OUR CREATOR and
Father, we thank you for making
men and women in your image. We enjoy
being with you in worship, and we are glad
that by your guidance and with your grace
we can find delight and enrichment in each
other. Help us, this day, to understand a little
more of the mystery of our nature and of the
relationship of men and women.

MOTHERS' UNION, ENGLAND

CHILDREN

$\mathcal{D}$EAR LORD, help me to keep my cool while I get the children off to school.

MARTHA GASH

GIVE ME PATIENCE and understanding with the children today. So much needs to be done to feed them all, and there's the washing, cleaning and shopping. Help me to realize that loving them and teaching them about you is much more important than a tidy home. Remind me to bite back the criticism and to praise whenever possible; to ask politely and to thank; to listen intently and answer carefully. I so often need your reminder—so nudge me, Lord!

KATHLEEN ANDREWS

*L*ORD, HOW CAN I THANK YOU for the wonderful gift of a new life, growing within me now? No praise is enough for the miracle that is happening to me. I know that my baby is developing day by day, and from the very tiniest beginnings is taking on the shape of the boy or girl, man or woman who will become my son or daughter.

Sometimes I find all this too much for me to imagine; but I want to understand your will and your ways, O Lord, and to thank you with my whole heart.

JOY HAWTHORNE

HELP US TO PREPARE a warm and peaceful home to welcome our child; teach us that it is not an abundance of worldly goods that will bring happiness, but that our constant love and patient care will surround our baby with all that is needed for his or her well being.

Give us your gifts of patience and gentleness, of understanding, love and peace, so that we may bring up a happy and contented child.

JOY HAWTHORNE

*L*ORD, YOU HAVE GIVEN US a
sacred trust to pass on our faith
in you to our children and grandchildren.
Give us, we pray, a gift from you that we may
do so with firm conviction and gentle trust,
believing that you will take our effort and use
it for your glory.

MAUREEN SUTTON

$\mathcal{H}$ELP US, LORD, to have patience with our children.

Help us. Lord, to recognize their difficulties and to help and guide them.

Help us to be tolerant of their untidiness.

Help us to teach them compassion and love toward their fellow beings.

Help them through the temptations that are presented to them in today's society.

SALISBURY DIOCESE, ENGLAND

*B*less and guard all fostered children
of all races and creeds and give them
reassurance in every situation. As they grow
up give them an understanding of the love
and concern there has been for them from
both their social workers and foster parents.

To those who care for them give wisdom,
compassion and an endless capacity for joyful
loving.

Dear God, above all give us all real concern
for these your children in the community,
and help us to take a share of caring for them
in whatever way we can.

SALISBURY DIOCESE, ENGLAND

*L*ORD GOD, WE OFFER TO YOU
the children living with only one
parent. Help them to feel your love, and be
with them in their times of confusion and
loneliness.

Give strength, patience and wisdom to the
parents trying to be both father and mother
to their children, at the same time as they
face up to their own needs.

Help us in the family of the church to be
open and caring with these families, as with
all the families we know.

CHRISTINE McMUILLEN

•••
49

*L*ORD, WE PRAY for young
people as they go out into the
world. Help them be strong and courageous
against the pressures and temptations of
daily life. Give them a clear vision, a sense
of rightness and grace to persevere.

PORTSMOUTH DIOCESE, ENGLAND

*L*OVING FATHER, we pray for homes which are no longer happy; where marriage and family life have broken down, where children are torn in their love and loyalties to parents, which causes them great distress. We pray for the counselors who try to ease these tensions; guide teachers and give them patience and understanding toward children who come from unhappy homes.

PORTSMOUTH DIOCESE, ENGLAND

O GOD, OUR HEAVENLY FATHER,
we pray for all young people in the
difficulties they face in their lives just "growing
up": relationships between the sexes; study and
exams; the choice of careers; leisure activities;
the search for employment. May we have
insight, patience and love in our dealings with
them, and we ask your blessing upon them as
they pass through this new, exciting part of
their lives.

CHELMSFORD DIOCESE, ENGLAND

O LORD, WE ASK your blessing
on our children who are married.
Grant them joy in their life together and a
love which grows deeper year by year. May
they rely upon your grace to guide and help
them at all times.

MOTHERS' UNION, ENGLAND

$\mathcal{D}$EAR LORD, I PRAY for the innocent babies who are born with a handicap. They may feel out of place, rejected and not wanted, but through friends and adults show them that you really love them, Lord, so that they grow knowing you faithfully.

KIGEZI DIOCESE, UGANDA

*G*OD, YOU MADE US ALL in your image and yet each of us is different and each has infinite value in your sight.

May we treasure our children as individuals in their own right. They have different skills, different personalities, different temperaments. Guide us as we nurture their skills, develop their personalities, understand their temperaments; that each may be whole, able to stand on his or her own, and strong in a living faith in the God who created them.

JOINED IN LOVE, NEW ZEALAND

CONNECTING WITH OTHERS

*L*ORD, YOU ARE WITH ME as I meet others. Give me your loving ways.

UNKNOWN

WE REMEMBER, LORD, those who have never had a word of kindness spoken to them. Give us that love which is patient and kind, that we may reach some cold heart today and warm it with some simple act of kindness.

JEAN COGGAN

FATHER, FORGIVE ME for looking the other way, for thinking that the things I have to do are more important than people. Forgive me for the many times I have not really listened, for the careless word spoken or the help not given; for the vain thoughts and hurtful silences, for any hurt I have inflicted unknowingly. Teach me to cross out the "I" and to seek only to follow you in word and action.

KITTY COOPER

*H*EAVENLY FATHER, you know the stresses and strains of modern life. We ask your blessing on those making a home together. May they have joy in their loving, tolerance and understanding in times of disagreement, security in the rush of daily living, and may they come to know the richness of your love.

BERYL DENNEY

*D*EAR FATHER GOD, please remember all elderly people; at home, in hospitals or in nursing homes. Be with them in their loneliness and anxiety, help them to overcome their difficulties; guide their friends and relatives to be tolerant, patient, understanding, caring and, above all, loving.

MARY PARSONS

A FRIEND CONFIDED her
anxieties to me today, Lord.
Help me to keep my mouth shut and my
heart and mind open to your guidance.
We both need your wisdom and love in her
situation and we know that if we ask, it will
be freely given.

BRENDA PREECE

*H*EAVENLY FATHER, be with us in our homes; bless our children, grandchildren, nieces, nephews and godchildren. Help us to set them a good example and never mislead them by our words and actions. When they bring us their secrets help us to listen with respect and understanding. Sometimes they seem to be far from us; help us to be wise and patient, and at all times to trust in you so they may see in us the difference it makes to live close to you and experience your love.

ELLA APPLETON

HEAVENLY FATHER, open our hearts to see the grudges that we bear against real and imagined hurts. Help us to be ready to listen when others ask our pardon. Help us to forgive those who do not ask for forgiveness; as you are ready to forgive us when we do wrong, even when we hurt you deeply.

RICKY CHILVERS

ALMIGHTY GOD, our Father in heaven, who is the source of comfort and strength, uplift our dying friend and her family. Give them all strength and faith to accept your way in the days to come. Grant that she may find an inner peace and understanding knowing that you are always with her.

MOTHERS' UNION, IRELAND

DEAR GOD, as we try to worship
you, help us through your Spirit
to be aware of opportunities to share the
knowledge of your love with those we meet
each day. Grant us the sensitivity to know
when to speak and when to be silent, and
above all to show forth your glory.

ST. ASAPH DIOCESE, WALES

*D*EAR LORD and heavenly Father, let not our lips be silent when others need our service, nor our hands be idle when they ask our aid. Let not our hearts be closed when others seek our love. May our minds be alert when our counsel is asked for.

Our hearts are yours, O Lord. May our praise and thanksgiving to you be in our service to others.

SUSIE M. PAYNE

FATHER, I BRING TO YOU in prayer people whose lives are starved of friendship: those who find it difficult to make friends; those who are cut off from their friends by distance; and those who in old age have lost the friends they had. Comfort and sustain them, O Lord, with your love.

CHELMSFORD DIOCESE, ENGLAND

$\mathcal{F}$ATHER, HELP US to help each other; teach us to be willing to do the small things just as gladly as those which are important. Help us to be good neighbors; may our words, our example and influence make life happier for those around us.

EUNICE DAVIES

O God, our heavenly Father, who does not want us, your children, to be in sorrow, come down now and be with our brothers and sisters who have lost their husbands or wives. Comfort them during their hard times, when they are alone at night or day; be with them to encourage and strengthen them. May they pass their days here on earth in the assurance that they will join you in your heavenly kingdom where there will be no more sorrow, weeping and pain.

RHODA ADE OLAREWAJU

COPING

$\mathcal{F}$ATHER, GIVE US STRENGTH to cope with the fast pace and the constant changes in our world today. Help us always to make the right decisions when needed. Give us compassion in our dealings with all people, particularly with those whose ways are different from ours. Give us your guidance in all we think, say and do; fill us with the power, the love and the joy of your Spirit.

MOTHERS' UNION, ENGLAND

O God, please help me to place myself and all my cares in your capable hands; help me to "let go" and accept your love and comfort at this stressful time. I know that often, quite wrongly, I feel that you are not aware of my needs especially when things do not happen as I wish, but such is my human failing.

Lord, you in your infinite wisdom and love are far-seeing; I know that you have a purpose for everyone and I must learn from you. If only I could always remember this and trust you more.

Help me to place myself in your loving hands, to always recognize and appreciate your goodness and mercy, so that when the cares and tribulations of this world try to take me over, please let me come to you to hear you say, "Peace. . .be still."

GLADYS DAVIES

*L*ORD, WHEN I AM AFRAID, please give me strength. When I am troubled, comfort me. If I am angry, calm my thoughts and when I feel ashamed, remind me of your forgiveness. When I am glad, let me remember your unfailing goodness to me. When my footsteps falter, walk beside me. When I forget you, as I often do, then Lord, forgive me, but do not forget me.

NORMA LETHBRIDGE

GOD, BE MY RESTING PLACE and my protection

In hours of trouble, defeat and dejection.

May I never give way to self-pity and sorrow,

May I always be sure of a better tomorrow.

May I stand undaunted come what may,

Secure in the knowledge I have only to pray

And ask my creator and Father above

To keep me serene in his grace and his love.

KITTY STREDDER

*H*ELP US LORD to know that you will never leave us to handle our problems alone. Help us to see how much you have done for us and to learn to worship and praise you. Help us Lord to see beyond the immediate difficulties and to pray to you for victory.

JANET NYENDA

FATHER, WE THANK YOU for
the knowledge that though weak
and helpless as we are, you are strong and
mighty. In your strength we can do all things.
Direct our course, we pray, and give us the
power to stop at no obstacle, but go through
victoriously to your praise and glory.

BO DIOCESE, SIERRA LEONE

LORD, when I feel myself sliding into the pit, stay close; sit with me in my silence and confusion, and give me your shoulder to lean on. Prevent me from falling too far, and in your good time, help me rise to my feet again.

BIRMINGHAM DIOCESE, ENGLAND

*H*oly Spirit, help and guide me. I don't know which choice to make: both are possible, and both are good. I want to know which is God's will. Help me to clear my mind so that I will see without prejudice; increase my love so that my choice will be guided by love of you. I am confused and need guidance. When, with your aid, I have chosen, stop me from looking back with regret and give me courage to go on fearlessly, trusting that I have done what is right and what is your will.

Mothers' Union, England

$\mathcal{P}$LEASE FATHER, TEACH ME
to understand the hard times
in my life; also prepare me for a life of
service to you. Help me to be realistic, but
not unreasonably fearful, in tackling any
assignment you give me.

JANET NYENDA

•••

*L*ORD, I FEEL SO ALONE—so desolate. Help me draw from you the strength to meet this day's fresh needs. Enable me to make decisions and give me the faith to put the future in your hands. May I find your everlasting joy and understand the purpose of sorrow.

BRENDA THORPE

GIVING
THANKS

O LORD MY GOD, as once again I open my eyes to the dawn of a new day, I thank you for the gift of sight to behold the wonderful things you have created all around us. I thank you for the gift of smell to appreciate the scent of the flowers in the gardens and fields, and for being able to touch and taste the fruits and vegetables you have provided for us.

I ask you to protect me from all the evils of this day and to guide me to do and say always what is right in your sight.

EDITH ELLIOT

O LORD, help us to be construction workers in the world of broken relationships. Let us work on bridges, not barricades, highways and not road blocks.

MOTHERS' UNION, ENGLAND

*W*E THANK YOU, LORD, for our families; and remember those who are lonely and have no loved ones.

We thank you for our homes; and pray for those who have no shelter.

We thank you for our work; and pray for those who are unemployed.

We thank you for our health; and pray for those who are sick in mind or body.

Dear Father, be with all of us in our various situations.

MOTHERS' UNION, ENGLAND

FATHER OF ALL, you showed us in word and deed that children are precious to you. Thank you for all that they bring to us; help us to nurture them in goodness.

KATE WATSON

*T*HANK YOU, GOD, for sunsets and trees; for roses and soft breezes; for birds and mountains, grass and fountains; for friends and quiet times; for your presence and strength in times of need. We thank you for all these things.

PAMELA MULLAN

Lord, how can I ever thank you for all you have done for me?

For the sheltering care and tenderness, and endless loyalty.

For all the paths your love has smoothed; the guidance from your hands,

The consolation of your Word in a world that misunderstands.

For the patience, Lord, you have had with me when I thought that I knew best,

For the sanctuary of your heart when I sorely needed rest,

The lamp of hope you held for me above dark ways and rough.

Oh how can I ever thank you Lord, or ever do enough?

GLADYS FINNIE

$\mathcal{P}$LEASE GOD, give me strength and courage to say the right things, to do the right things, never to be afraid or do anything silly, and to thank you for each day.

OLIVE JACKSON

PRAYERS FOR WORLD PEACE

$\mathcal{D}$EAR LORD, WE PRAY for those who lead, for those who have power, and for those who train and influence others. May they seek your wisdom, your will and your honor in fulfilling their responsibilities, especially in working for peace.

CHRIST CHURCH, LONDON

...
91

$\mathcal{D}$EAR HEAVENLY FATHER, we bring before you all the nations of your world who are not at peace. We pray that leaders may be influenced by your love and learn to live together without war. We pray for those actively involved in fighting and ask you to comfort their families. We pray for children in war-torn countries; inspire the rest of us around your world to do all we can to rehabilitate these little children.

MAUREEN LIMBRICK

*A*LMIGHTY AND everlasting God, heavenly Father, we thank you for your great love to us. I pray you to change the hearts of those who like their problems to be solved in the way of war. By killing innocent people all over the world and making themselves glad when destroying most of the important places, they have forgotten you.

YODITA ELISA

D EAR LORD, you have taught us to
love our enemies and to do good to
those who hate us. We pray for all terrorists.
Take from their hearts all evil thoughts and
help them to see that the power of love is
stronger than the bomb and the bullet. Lead
them from violence into your ways of peace.

ROCHESTER DIOCESE, ENGLAND